Tonight's Concert

Using Data and Graphs

Consultants

Pamela Dase, M.A.Ed.
National Board Certified Teacher

Barbara Talley, M.S.
Texas A&M University

Publishing Credits

Dona Herweck Rice, *Editor-in-Chief*
Robin Erickson, *Production Director*
Lee Aucoin, *Creative Director*
Timothy J. Bradley, *Illustration Manager*
Sara Johnson, M.S.Ed., *Senior Editor*
Aubrie Nielsen, M.S.Ed., *Associate Education Editor*
Jennifer Kim, M.A.Ed., *Associate Education Editor*
Neri Garcia, *Senior Designer*
Stephanie Reid, *Photo Editor*
Rachelle Cracchiolo, M.S.Ed., *Publisher*

Teacher Created Materials

5301 Oceanus Drive
Huntington Beach, CA 92649-1030
http://www.tcmpub.com
ISBN 978-1-4333-3464-1
© 2012 Teacher Created Materials, Inc.

Table of Contents

Behind the Scenes

Have you ever seen a live concert? There is nothing quite like a big crowd singing along and cheering for a band. The lighting, costumes, dance routines, and of course, the music, all work together to make a great show.

Booking Agents

Concert tour managers have to work closely with booking agents. Booking agents are the people who arrange to use the stadiums or arenas where the band will perform while on tour.

I know a lot about big concerts in large **venues** (VEN-yooz). For 20 years, I have been working as a concert tour manager. My job is to organize all the details that are involved in getting a band to play many shows at a variety of locations. Some of our tours have gone around the country, and some have traveled around the globe! You may be surprised at all the work that goes on behind the scenes of a music concert.

Who Are the Fans?

My first task is to get to know the band and what kind of music they perform. It is also my job to know the **demographic** (dem-uh-GRAF-ik) that is most dedicated to seeing the band onstage. That tells me who their fans might be and what types of locations might be best for the tour. Some musicians, for example, may easily fill a small venue that allows only adults to attend. Other artists might draw large crowds of fans of all ages and need larger venues.

Some musicians may be famous in one region but unfamiliar to people in another. Some bands have fans of all ages from all over the world. Those are the types of bands that kids can listen to with their parents and their grandparents.

Demographics of fans, venues, and target audiences are all important in planning a tour.

To plan a concert, a tour manager looked at the results of a survey of 350 people from 10–49 years old. The survey asked whether or not they were likely to attend a concert featuring the group that was touring. After he collected the data, he separated the people into groups by age. He displayed the data on the **histogram** below.

Concert Interest by Age

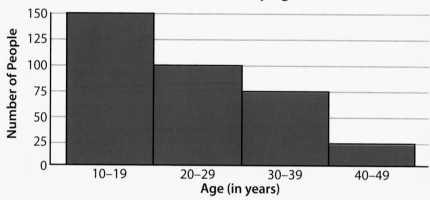

a. What **interval** did the tour manager use to represent the ages on the histogram?

b. The first interval is 10–19 years. How many people in that age group said they would likely attend the concert?

c. Toward which age group would you target the concert?

Planning the Show

A lot of planning is done before a concert tour starts. Once we realize what kinds of fans will be coming to see the band, we want to give them the best show possible.

I help the band decide what songs to include in their **set list**. They think about the songs they like to play. They also think about the songs that their fans will want to hear. Those may be songs that are popular and currently on the radio. The band may also have some big hits from the past that they want to include.

Choreographing Moves

A choreographer (kohr-ee-OG-ruh-fer) is a person who creates dance routines. Many musicians work with choreographers when planning movements and dance steps for their shows.

Some bands want only to play their music and have a good time. Others have ideas about dance routines, lighting, videos, and other **effects** to add to the excitement of the show. Some musicians work with professionals to add all these elements to the live performance.

LET'S EXPLORE MATH

This histogram shows the same data as the histogram on page 7. The size of the intervals has been changed.

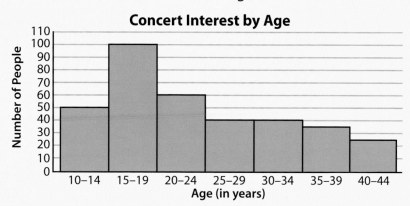

a. What size interval did the tour manager use for this histogram?

b. How did changing the interval give the tour manager more information about the concert attendance?

One element in planning a show is thinking about the length of the performance. Timing is important for a couple of reasons. The venue managers need to know the length of the band's performance. If there is an opening act before the band plays, the length of that set is included, too. The venue may have rules for how late a concert may go. To determine the length of the show, we have to account for all the songs being played. We must also think about whether the band will need a break. They will likely come out for at least one **encore** (AHN-kohr) after the last song is played.

mixing console

Lip Sync

Some performers like putting on elaborate shows with many costume changes and energetic dance numbers. To make it easier to maintain a high level of energy in their performance, the singers may choose to lip sync. That means they are singing along to a previously-recorded version of the song. Some fans do not like that because they prefer to hear a live performance at a concert rather than a recorded one.

Emily investigated the length of 20 concerts for her favorite band. She found the following lengths, in minutes: 85, 102, 117, 150, 92, 128, 122, 75, 130, 132, 103, 125, 82, 120, 135, 126, 121, 90, 145, 138.

a. What are the maximum and minimum numbers of minutes for a concert?

b. To graph this data, what would be a good interval to use for the number of minutes?

c. Make a histogram to display the data.

d. Using your graph, what do you think would be a likely amount of time to expect for the length of a concert by this band?

The timing of a performance is also important for the rest of the crew. The lighting crew, for example, needs to know the length and order of the songs being played. The lights are designed to **enhance** a specific song and must be timed accurately

The Cost of a Concert

One reason we plan our concerts so well is because we do not want to disappoint any of the fans. They come to a show expecting to see and hear something exciting. They also may be paying a lot of money for this special event.

Concert tickets have definitely become more expensive over the years. Some bands can still play in smaller venues. That helps to keep the costs down. When popular bands play in large settings, like a stadium or an arena, fans will likely pay a lot for tickets to see a show.

We always try to reach out to fans who do not have a lot of money. We work with local radio stations to give away tickets. We also record our live performances and sell the DVDs. That way, people can hear live music by the band even if they cannot attend a live concert.

Walt Disney Concert Hall

LET'S EXPLORE MATH

A band has increased the price of tickets each year over the last five years. The two **line graphs** show the ticket prices from 2007–2011. A line graph is a graph that shows change over time.

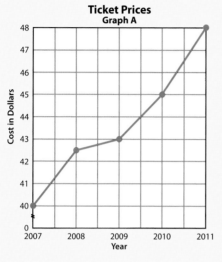

Ticket Prices
Graph A

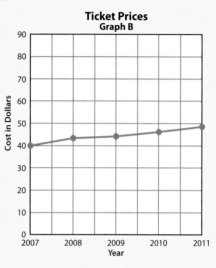

Ticket Prices
Graph B

a. What was the ticket price each year? Does it matter which line graph you use?

b. Why do the two graphs look so different when they represent the same information?

The price of a ticket is not the only cost for a concertgoer. That is just the cost to get in the door!

First, fans have to pay to get to the concert venue. Some fans take public transportation. They may want to avoid driving in traffic or high parking costs.

Before the show, some fans may want to buy refreshments. Concession (kuhn-SESH-uhn) stands sell everything from ice cream to hot dogs to sodas. They bring in a lot of money when an event attracts thousands of fans.

Finally, some concertgoers may want to buy a souvenir (soo-vuh-NEER) as a way to remember the event. Concert T-shirts are always popular items to buy at a show. Posters, stickers, programs, and CDs are all typically available at a large concert.

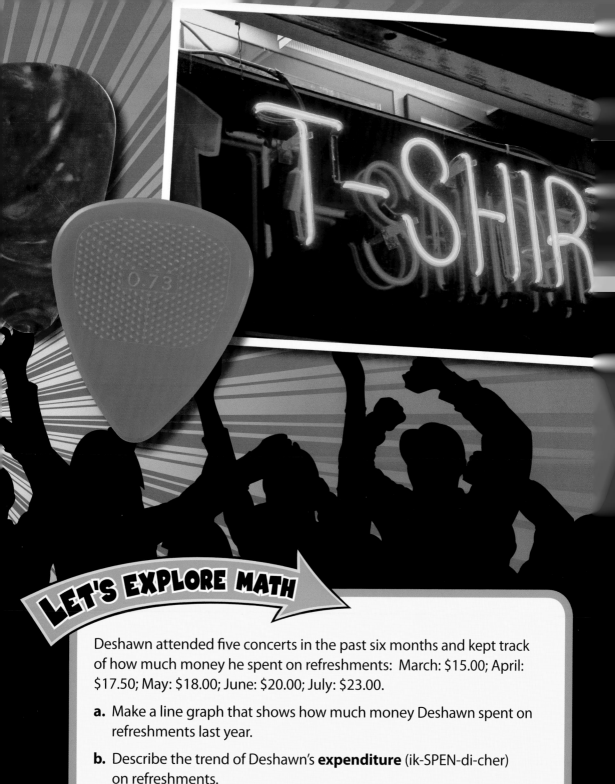

Deshawn attended five concerts in the past six months and kept track of how much money he spent on refreshments: March: $15.00; April: $17.50; May: $18.00; June: $20.00; July: $23.00.

a. Make a line graph that shows how much money Deshawn spent on refreshments last year.

b. Describe the trend of Deshawn's **expenditure** (ik-SPEN-di-cher) on refreshments.

Some fans might look at the total cost to see a show and decide that it is too expensive. They may try to see the band at a free show, but free shows are pretty rare. Many fans wonder why concert ticket prices are so high.

road crew

sound board

The Crew

I can tell you that bands do not like to charge fans too much money to see them perform. Yet big concerts require a crew of hundreds of professionals, so a lot of the money spent on tickets goes toward the salaries for those people. They make it possible for the show to go on.

Who are these concert employees? Sometimes they are called *roadies*, which is a slang term for road crew. The road crew includes all the people who help the band get from place to place and prepare for performances onstage.

sound technician

Some bands travel on tour buses.

Many different people help behind the scenes of a concert. Large shows need a large crew to make everything run smoothly.

I get to know a lot of the crew on tour because I travel with the band from city to city. I make sure that the crew members all get their jobs done. I also take care of all the details necessary to move both the band and the crew from city to city. There are a lot of people and equipment to move each day.

Not Just for Concerts

Stage managers are found in all types of productions. Plays, ballets, and operas all require a stage manager.

Some of the most important crew members on concert tours are the stage managers. They are in charge of organizing the concert itself. Everything that happens onstage is their responsibility. They handle details between the musicians and the different crews that work on the concert, like the backstage crew.

Stage managers are in charge of the various workers who help with the concert itself. There are **technicians** (tek-NISH-uhnz) for every kind of instrument. A guitar technician is responsible for testing the guitars during the soundcheck—the time before the show starts when the instruments are tuned and checked to see if any maintenance (MEYN-tuh-nuhns) is needed. There may be different technicians for other instruments, such as keyboards and drums, or one technician may be responsible for all of them.

The instrument technicians work closely with the sound engineers. Together, they make sure that all the instruments sound the way they should.

Lighting technicians are key members of the road crew, as well. They work with sound engineers to plan a lighting show to accompany the songs being played.

guitar technician

A **bar graph** is a graph that displays quantities using vertical or horizontal bars. It has a title and horizontal and vertical **axes**, which are labeled. A **scale** is used to show the **frequency** of the data. The scale runs along the side or bottom of the graph, depending on the direction of the bars.

LET'S EXPLORE MATH

The tour manager for the group wants to reduce the personal expenses on the road of all the band members. He presented a **circle graph** and bar graph to show their expenses. Use each graph to answer the questions below.

Expenditures on the Road Circle Graph

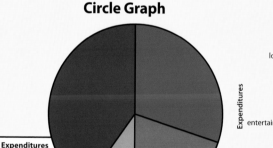

Expenditures
- lodging
- food
- entertainment
- transportation

Expenditures on the Road Bar Graph

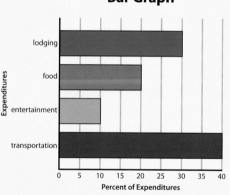

a. Name two expenditures where one is about twice the other.

b. Name two expenditures where one is about one-third of the other.

c. Which graph is more useful for a quick impression of how the expenditures are divided up?

d. Which graph is more useful for estimating the percent spent on a category?

e. What scale is used on the bar graph for percent of expenditures?

f. If you were the manager, which category do you think could be reduced? Why?

Getting the Word Out

As the tour manager, I feel a huge sense of responsibility to my band and crew. I certainly want the band to be popular, but I also want the band's concerts to be a success for all the people who work behind the scenes.

One of the best ways to help make a concert a success is to **promote** the band before and during a tour. That means making sure people know about the band and its tour schedule.

One easy way to promote a band is to have an online presence. That is essential for any band or musician who wants to reach a large audience. Promoting, sharing, and selling music online are ways that many music lovers discover new music.

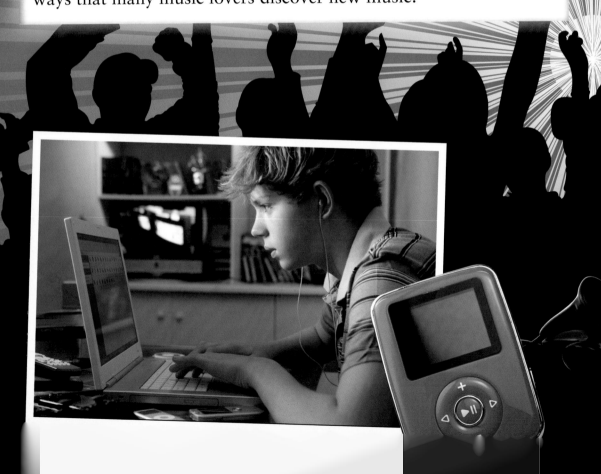

The band is hoping to get its music included in a popular online music store. They surveyed some fans to find out how many of the band's songs their fans would likely download. The tour manager organized the responses with a **line plot**. A line plot, also known as a dot plot, is a number line diagram that uses an *x* or other mark to show the frequencies of items or categories being tallied.

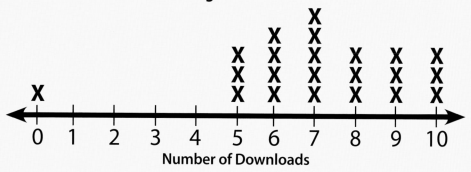

Song Downloads

Number of Downloads

a. What does each *x* represent?

b. What do the numbers along the horizontal axis represent?

I have a role in promoting the band as well. I am responsible for getting the band members to talk to the media. I schedule television and radio interviews in different cities that we visit. The goal is for fans to see or hear that the band is playing a live show in town and decide to come to the performance. Sometimes the group will even play a song during the interview to give fans a sample of what they will hear at the concert.

Benefit Concerts

Typically the proceeds from concert ticket sales go to pay band members and to cover concert costs. Occasionally, a band or musician will agree to perform at a benefit concert. In that case, fans buy tickets but the proceeds go to a charitable organization or cause rather than to the band.

Promotional interviews can include both the headlining band and the opening act. If the opening act is less familiar to fans than the headlining band, these interviews can be a great way for people to learn about the band. In some cases, the opening act may have a strong fan base that can attract a larger audience to the show.

Enjoy the Show!

Seeing a band live in concert is an amazing experience! I have toured with many groups and I still get excited when the lights go out and the crowd roars. Enjoying a performance together with a group of people who have similar musical tastes is something that everyone should experience.

What many people do not think about when they watch a live show is all the hard work that goes into making that show a success. The next time you go to a concert, think about the engineers and technicians. Look for a lighting crew member or a stage manager. Maybe you will see me running around to be sure that everything is running smoothly. We are all doing our best to ensure that you enjoy a good show.

The largest concert ever was held on New Year's Eve in 1994 on Copacabana Beach in Brazil. Singer Rod Stewart performed for a crowd of 3,500,000 people!

PROBLEM-SOLVING ACTIVITY

The Tour Manager's Assistant

The band Lucky Ducky has just closed a show and is heading for the next stop on its concert tour. Lucky Ducky's tour manager needs to order items for the souvenir stands at future shows and wants to review the sales from past concerts. You are her assistant and need to present the data to her. The table below shows the number of each item sold from the past five cities on the tour.

Souvenir	Number Sold
hat	405
T-shirt	1,150
sweatshirt	960
beach towel	315
bracelet	1,570
CD	695
DVD	285

Solve It!

a. What type of graph would you create to show how many of each type of souvenir was sold? Why?

b. Create a graph to show to the tour manager that would best display the data.

c. The tour manager loves line plots and wants you to make a line plot to show how many of each type of souvenir was sold. Write an explanation to tell him why a line plot would not be the best way to display this data.

Use the steps below to help you answer the questions.

Step 1: Choose a graph (histogram, line graph, line plot, bar graph, circle graph) that would best show the data for souvenir sales.

Step 2: Create the graph. Remember to give the graph a title and label the axes (if applicable).

Step 3: Think about the number of marks you would have to make to show the number of bracelets that were sold. Write a paragraph that explains why a line plot is not the best graph for this set of data.

Glossary

axes—horizontal or vertical lines from which distances are measured on a coordinate grid

bar graph—a graph in which quantities are represented by bars

circle graph—a graph that displays data as sections of a circle (also known as a pie chart)

demographic—the characteristics of a human population or a part of it

effects—special visual or sound features in a stage production or movie

encore—an additional or repeated performance in response to audience demand

enhance—to improve or add value to something

expenditure—payment for goods or services

frequency—the number of times something occurs

histogram—a bar graph that represents the frequency of data within a data set using adjacent bars

interval—the distance between numbers from one grid line to another on a graph

line graphs—graphs that show change over time

line plot—a number line diagram that uses an x or other mark to show the frequencies of items or categories being tallied (also known as a dot plot)

promote—to make people aware through advertising

scale—a system of marks at fixed intervals on a graph that are labeled with numbers

set list—a list of songs that a band intends to play during a performance

technicians—specialists in the technical details of a job

venues—places where events, such as concerts, are held

Index

Let's Explore Math

Page 7:

a. 10 years

b. 150 people

c. 10–19 years old

Page 9:

a. 5 years

b. This graph shows that the 10–14 group is not as important as the 15–19 group. The most important 10-year age group would be 15–24.

Page 11:

a. Maximum: 150 minutes; Minimum: 75 minutes

b. One possible answer: 20 minutes

c. One possible answer:

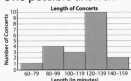

d. 120–139 minutes

Page 13:

a. 2007: $40; 2008: $42.50; 2009: $43; 2010: $45; 2011: $48. No; The graphs display the same information.

Page 13 (cont.)**:**

b. The graphs look different because the interval (scale) is different for the cost in dollars.

Page 15:

a.

b. Deshawn spends more money each month on refreshments.

Page 21:

a. food and entertainment, or transportation and food

b. entertainment and lodging

c. circle graph

d. bar graph

e. 5%

f. Answers will vary.

Page 23:

a. 1 fan

b. The horizontal axis numbers represent different numbers of downloads.

Problem-Solving Activity

a. A bar graph is the best way to display the large numbers of souvenirs sold because you can adjust the frequency interval to make a manageable graph.

b.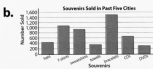

c. Answers should address the fact that line plots are not the best graph to display this data because the number of marks needed would be far too great.